United States Infantry Europe 1942-45

by Howard P.Davies
Series Editor Brian L.Davis

Published by
Arco Publishing Company, Inc.,
219 Park Avenue South
New York, N.Y. 10003.

Library of Congress Catalog
Card Number 73-83740
ISBN 0—668—03361—4
Printed in Great Britain
Series Editor: Brian L. Davis, for
Key Military Publications
Series Design: David Gibbons, for
Arms and Armour Press
Typesetting: ABCDesign
Camerawork: Duotech
Graphics Limited

Printed in England

Acknowledgements
The author acknowledges with
thanks the invaluable assistance
given by Brian L. Davis in the
preparation of this book. All the
illustrations are US Official
photographs, reproduced by kind
permission of the Imperial War
Museum, London.

Plate 1, below: *Men of the
80th US Infantry Division,
3rd US Army, with their vehicles
and material in a landing craft
during the process of crossing
the Rhine at Mainz in March
1945.*

Contents

Historical Background

Germany declared war on the United States of America on 11th December 1941. Prior to that date the United States had given Britain great support in the form of Lend-Lease — support which was of such magnitude as to be only just short of war itself. In Britain many Americans had already come forward voluntarily to offer their services to the forces of the British Crown. Many wore the uniform of the Royal Air Force, both flying and maintaining aircraft. Even a Home Guard unit of Americans was formed in July 1940 by a First World War US veteran resident in the United Kingdom, Brigadier-General W.H.Hayes.

Early in 1940 the US Army numbered some 265,000 men; by mid-1941 its strength had increased to some one and a half million men. On 26th January 1942, just 46 days after entering the war, the first American infrantrymen arrived in Northern Ireland under the command of Major-General Russell P. Hartle and a programme of intensive training was put into effect. By September 1942 Major-General Mark Clark, Commander of the United States Ground Forces in the European theatre of operations. (ETO), had established his headquarters in England. At a Thanksgiving Day service held on 26th November 1942 in Westminster Abbey the Stars and Stripes were unfurled above the ancient building for the first time in its long history.

Early in 1943 a training centre for American officers was set up in England, and for some of its personnel this was a return visit. One such man was Lieutenant-General William H. Simpson who had served as Chief of Staff of the United States 33rd Division of the American Expeditionary Force in 1918. General Eisenhower arrived in England from North Africa in January of 1944 to take up his duties as Supreme Commander for the forthcoming invasion of Europe, codeword 'Overlord'. This stupendous operation was launched in the early hours of 6th June 1944 when an armada of some 5,000 vessels, unprecedented in military history, sailed into the pre-dawn darkness of the English Channel.

By nightfall on the first day — 'D-Day' — the 1st US Infantry Division was expected to form part of a force having a beachhead 16 miles wide and about 6 miles deep. However, it was only by sheer hard slogging that the 1st Division, by the end of the first long day, had succeeded in gaining the line of the coastal road. It had seemed earlier that the leading waves of infantry would be broken and beaten; but at the critical moment the troops responded to the fine example of leadership shown by Colonel G.A.Taylor, and the first small parties had made the break after being pinned down on the beach.

On the next day, 7th June — D-Day + 1 — Omaha beach was still being heavily shelled and mortared by the Germans. The landing points were so cluttered up with wreckage of stores and human bodies that the greatest difficulties were experienced in landing further supplies to the hard pressed troops. The shelling and mortaring only began to subside later in the day when the 1st Infantry Division gained ground to the south.'Bloody Omaha', the name given to this part of the Normandy landing area,was indeed no flippant sobriquet.

By the evening of 11th June the 1st US Infantry Division was 14 miles south of Omaha beach and had drawn level with the British force battling hard to capture Tilly. The American forces now began to make progress inland, pushing forward towards St.Lô and across the Cotentin peninsula to cut off Cherbourg. By 18th June the Americans were across the Cotentin, and turning towards Cherbourg, and on 10th July St. Lô fell to the advance elements of the United States 29th Infantry Division.

2. Left: *A US infantry private, his trumpet strapped securely to his battle equipment, leaves a British embarkation port with American reinforcements for the French beachhead. Reinforcements of men and material were poured steadily into France both by air and by sea immediately following the initial Allied Normandy Landings of 6th June 1944.*

In the meantime the 4th US Infantry Division had, on 24th June, reached the coast 3 miles east of Cherbourg, but all initial attempts to penetrate into the city itself were thwarted. However, by the evening of the 26th all organised opposition there had collapsed and the Americans were swarming through the streets.

About this time operation 'Cobra' was planned. This was the codeword for the operation to bring about the break-out from the Carentan area into Normandy. By diverting the 17.SS-Panzer-Grenadier-Division Götz von Berlichingen after the capture of Carentan by the Americans, Field Marshal Rommel left undefended the next objective for the 1st US Infantry — Caumont. Standing atop a steep hill, Caumont strategically dominated the surrounding countryside, and the Germans were fully aware of its significance. The commander of the 84th German Army Corps, General Erich Marcks, himself set out for Caumont in an attempt to improvise a temporary garrison to hold the town, but was killed on the road by fighter bombers of the US Army Air Force before he could intervene. By the time German headquarters knew of his fate any further action to try and hold Caumont was futile and by the morning of the next day the town was in American hands.

Operation 'Cobra' now began to take effect: the 4th US Infantry Division took the centre, with the 9th US Infantry Division and the 30th US Infantry Division on the right and left respectively. On 7th August the 30th Division was holding and checking the Germans around Mortain, and a part of the 4th Division was deployed to seal off the deep penetration in the centre. At dawn on 25th August 1944 the French from the west and the Americans from the south began driving for the heart of Paris.

Meanwhile, on the south coast of France the 7th US Army landed near St. Tropez on 15th August 1944 and reached the German defence line south of Belfort. After battling across France the Americans now prepared for a heavy assault in the Aachen area of the German border. On 2nd November 1944 the 28th US Infantry Division — the 'Keystone' division — attacked through the Huertgen forest on the south east of the

3. Below: *A flamethrower team under instruction at an assault training centre for the US Army 'somewhere in Britain', November 1943. In preparation for the forthcoming invasion of German occupied Europe, units of the US Army Assault Section carried out a number of extensive exercises in the United Kingdom. Using live ammunition, these operations included training for the establishment of a bridgehead on an 'enemy-occupied' beach and attacks, supported by aircraft and artillery, on enemy 'hedgehog' positions.*

town. Their objective was the town of Schmidt, which was another of those strategically important places on high ground. The German forces in this sector fought with the utmost tenacity in view of the great strategic importance of the area, and also the fact that they were now called upon to defend their very homeland against an invading enemy. The fierce battle that ensued cost the 28th Infantry over 6,000 casualties. The divisional insignia of the 28th took the form of a red keystone, the shape and colour of their badge having earned them the title of the 'bloody bucket' division; in this instance it was grimly appropriate. By December 1944, the fighting for the Huertgen forest had cost the American forces 24,000 men killed, missing, captured or wounded.

Mid-December saw the final German attempt to halt the inexorable advance of the Allies. In an effort to cut the Allied forces in two they launched their last reserves against the weakest point of the Allied lines in the final campaign that has come to be known as the Ardennes Offensive or the 'Battle of the Bulge'. From Monschau to Luxembourg the vast German attack gathered momentum and, taking the American forces completely by surprise, was successful in pushing them back through the Ardennes Forest. In the Schnee Eifel area two inexperienced regiments of the 106th US Infantry Division, which had only just arrived in Europe, having landed at Le Harve on 6th December, were quickly outflanked and completely encircled early in the morning of 17th December.

In the south the battered 28th US Infantry Division was 'resting', with its three regiments holding a twenty-seven mile front at Bastogne. In spite of great hardship the men in besieged Bastogne held on, and although surrounded by the Germans they did not give in. Bastogne was relieved on 28th December, and by New Year's Day 1945 it was painfully evident to the German command that the operation had failed — but only just. The Germans had so very nearly reached their main objective — Antwerp. The 'bulge' created by the German offensive was now inexorably reduced, and by the end of January it had been flattened out. The Germans were back where they had started, on their own borders.

The cost to the Americans was in the region of 81,000 casualties. In an address before the House of Commons, Winston Churchill, in reference to the Ardennes offensive said 'This has been the greatest American battle of the war and will, I believe, be regarded as an ever famous American victory'.

The 30th US Infantry Division was engaged in the assault across the river Rhine at Wesel and by dawn on 24th March 1945 its infantrymen were holding three bridgeheads and beginning to move forward. During the night of March 22nd-23rd 1945 six battalions of the 5th US Infantry Division crossed the Rhine at Oppenheim, south of Mainz, at the cost of only eight men killed and twenty wounded. On the evening of 23rd, the US Infantry in this sector already held a bridgehead 6 miles deep and 7 miles wide. Between the end of January and the beginning of May 1945 the American forces battled their way across Germany: the United States 9th Army from north of Aachen to the river Elbe near Magdeburg; the 1st US Army from the Aachen area to the Halle-Leipzig sector; the 3rd US Army dividing its target between Chemnitz in mid-Germany and Linz in the south; and the 7th US Army advancing from the Saar towards the Brenner Pass in Austria. On April 25th 1945 the first American patrol came into contact with the 175th Russian Rifle Regiment at Strehla on the river Elbe. By 8th May 1945 the war in Europe was over.

Although every item of American military clothing was carefully designed and manufactured, rigorously tested with a great deal of emphasis laid on the correct method of wearing the uniform by the individual, the overall impression made by the US fighting soldier both in the United Kingdom and in Europe was one of relaxed formality.

By comparison with the British military dress, especially the Battle Dress in use at that time, the American uniforms appeared far more attractive both in their cut and in the material used. The US M1 steel helmet afforded the wearer a far greater degree of protection than the British pattern helmet and American combat clothing was better suited to training and frontline conditions than that used initially by the British.

Between the time that the first US troops arrived in the United Kingdom (January 1942) and the end of the war in Europe (May 1945) many new, and in some cases modified, forms of military clothing were introduced. This rapid development of new uniform and clothing for wear by the American fighting soldier resulted in a wide range of dress in use in the European theatre of operations. Added to this were the numerous individuals who, for the sake of comfort, adapted their clothing and equipment to suit their individual whims.

The Purpose and Importance of the Military Uniform

The wearing of the prescribed uniform identified the officer or soldier as a member of the Army of the United States. Insignia worn upon the uniform in a prescribed manner indicated the arm of service, grade, and other data, such as awards of decorations, service medals and badges, and assignment to a tactical unit. It was — and still is — unlawful for any person not in the military service to wear the uniform as a whole or any component which had been designated as an official part of the uniform. In time of war, in case of capture by an enemy, the wearing of the official uniform entitled the officer or soldier to receive preferential treatment as a prisoner of war in a manner agreed upon between nations. The colour, design, style and materials from which the many items of uniform clothing were authorised to be manufactured were prescribed by regulations. There was also sufficient variety in the types of uniform to satisfy conditions in different climates, weather conditions, and service necessities as to duty performed.[1]

The Manner of Wearing the Uniform

The uniforms of officers and men were required to conform, both on and off duty, in every respect to the specifications therefor and to be worn in the prescribed manner. In particular the following points were to be observed in wearing the uniform
1. The uniform was to be kept clean and neat and in good repair.
2. Missing insignia and buttons were to be promptly replaced.
3. Insignia and buttons on the service uniform during peace were to be a bright finish; in war they were to have a dull bronze finish.
4. Overcoats, coats and shirts were to be worn buttoned throughout.
6. Service hats were to be worn in regulation shape. It will be seen from some of the photographs reproduced in this work that these requirements were not always fulfilled, especially un-under combat conditions.

---

[1] Dress uniforms used by officers and generals of the Army are not dealt with in this work. Nor are uniforms in use by Army Air Force personnel, despite its being during the Second World War, part of the US Army.

Commanding officers were ordered to see that all officers and men had uniforms as prescribed, in accordance with the regulations. They were required to inspect the service uniforms, arms, and field equipment of personnel under their respective commands as often as they deemed necessary in order to assure themselves that all members thereof were prepared to take the field upon short notice, fully uniformed and equipped, as prescribed in the regulations.

Wearing Uniforms after a Change in Design

Whenever changes in design or material of uniforms were published in *Army Regulations* (AR 600-35) all members of the Army were authorised to wear out existing clothing. Uniforms procured or manufactured after promulgation of the changes were to be of the new type. Whereas enlisted men were issued with all the uniforms, clothing and equipment required by their rank and necessary for the performance of their duty, officers were required to provide at their own expense many articles of uniform and uniform equipment. However, certain items, such as steel helmets, were regulation issue to all ranks of the Army.

Officers to be in the Same Uniform as Troops

Officers on duty with or attached in any capacity to troops were to wear the corresponding uniform prescribed for troops. Exceptions were being permitted to wear the woollen uniform when the troops were in cotton, or vice versa.

Kinds of Uniforms

There were many kinds of individual uniforms, each designed for a definite purpose, which were required or authorised to be worn. The wool service uniform may be said to be the only one that was required to be in the possession of all personnel of the Army of the United States. The cotton service uniform was prescribed for summer wear. Officers were privileged to wear the woollen uniform if they wished to do so, while the troops were in cotton. The several uniforms were as follows:

Service Uniforms:
1. The wool service uniform with coat.
2. The wool service uniform with olive-drab shirt.
3. The cotton service uniform with cotton or wool olive-drab shirt.

Work (Fatigue) Uniform
Olive-drab, herringbone twill.

Combat Dress:[1]
This varied according to the types of dress introduced at different times and the circumstances and conditions under which it was worn. It was authorised for wear by all combat personnel and as such was identical for all ranks, the only distinguishing feature being the insignia of rank (if any) displayed by the wearer.

The Service Uniform

The uniform for wear in the performance of duty was the ser-

---

[1] The term 'combat dress' or 'combat clothing' refers to uniforms worn not only in the fighting zone but also during field training and manoeuvres. This work includes details of certain items of dress worn by medics from US infantry units as well as items of US Military Police clothing.

vice uniform of which there were two kinds, the woollen and the cotton. The woollen uniform was prescribed for wear by the commanding officer when the climate or weather did not require the cotton uniform.

The Service Uniform, Arms and Equipment for Officers, Warrant Officers and Enlisted Men:
The articles listed below were prescribed for habitual wear by all officers, warrant officers and enlisted men, unless otherwise prescribed.

When Dismounted:
Officers' or warrant officers belt (optional) or the cloth belt was permitted to be worn. (The cloth belt was only used by enlisted men and was optional for officers and warrant officers.)
Service cap, except when other headgear was prescribed or authorised.
Service coat, except when shirt without coat was authorised.
Decorations, service medals, and badges as prescribed or authorised.
Gloves.
Necktie.
Service ribbons, optional.
Shirt.
Army russet leather shoes, except when boots were authorised.
Plain tan or brown socks when low shoes were worn.
Identification tags.
Service trousers, except when breeches were authorised.

When Mounted:
When mounted the Army russet leather shoes and service trousers were replaced by breeches, boots and spurs; the rest of the uniform remained as for dismounted duty.

For Wear on Field Duty when Dismounted:
All officers, warrant officers and enlisted men were required to wear the following articles:
Garrison cap (the former 'overseas' or 'field' cap), except when the service hat or other headgear was prescribed or authorised.
Service coat, or field jacket, except when the shirt without coat was authorised.
Canvas leggins, except when boots were authorised.
Service ribbons, optional.
Service shirt.
Tie, worn with the service coat. Field jacket worn buttoned up at the neck.
High Army russet leather shoes.
Identification tags.
Service trousers.
Web field equipment. (This varied according to type of combat/field duty performed.)
Pistol (Usually worn by officers and warrant officers.)

For Wear on Field Duty when Mounted:
The same articles were worn as stated above for wear dismounted, omitting the leggins, shoes and trousers, and adding service breeches, boots, spurs and leather gloves when prescribed.

The Work Uniform for Officers and Enlisted Men
The work uniform could be worn either over or without the Service Uniform. In all cases, insignia of grade and arm or service was to be worn as prescribed for the olive-drab shirt. The

4, 5. Security guards at the American Army Headquarters in London wore distinctive items of uniform dress: white painted helmet liners, white gloves, leggins and belts with cross straps were worn, together with the regulation issue winter service uniform.
The US Army Military Police (shown here wearing winter service uniform) wore in addition to the issue uniform a white belt, white leggins, gloves and white painted helmets or liners. The use of white helmets by the Military Police with their MP markings gave rise to their nickname of 'Snowdrops'.

work uniform was provided for wear on duty in the performance of which the clothing worn could have become soiled or unsightly. It was permitted to be worn for drill and combat training (plate 21) and when participating in field exercises and manoeuvres. The articles comprising the work uniform were as follows:

Herringbone twill cap.

Gloves, when conditions required them.

Herringbone twill hat (although other authorised headgear could be worn when climatic or service conditions were deemed to make this advisable).

Service shoes.

One-piece herringbone twill suit (or jacket and trousers, herringbone twill).

Identification tags.

The herringbone twill cap and the herringbone twill suit were worn by personnel of the armoured forces and by mechanics only of the other arms and services. The herringbone twill hat, jacket and trousers were worn by all other personnel.(For the differences between these articles of uniform see pages 18-21.)

Combat Uniforms for Officers, Warrant Officers and Enlisted Men

As already stated this form of dress varied according to the type of uniform items introduced at different times and the circumstances and conditions under which they were worn. Full details regarding the individual items that went to make up the various forms of combat uniforms as well as details of the various service uniforms and work uniforms are dealt with on the following pages.

The Winter Service Coat

The winter service coat (part of the winter service uniform) was a prescribed article of the uniform of wool, elastique, olive-drab (dark shade), 18-26ounce. It was prescribed for wear by all personnel of the United States Army (plates 4,5). All coats were to be buttoned throughout whenever worn. The buttons of the service coat, except for officers of the Corps of Engineers bore the coat-of-arms of the United States. Shoulder loops (shoulder straps) and lapel insignia, decorations, service medals and badges were worn with the service coat.

Officers' Tunic Belts

Belts of two types were worn by officers. They were the officers' belt, M1921 (the 'Sam Browne' belt) of Army russet leather and brass trimmings with a single shoulder cross strap; and the officer's cloth belt, which matched the coat in colour and fabric. This was 1¾inches in width, equipped with a removable brass or olive-drab plastic 1¾inch tongueless buckle and had a tapered end. The officer's belt, M1921, or the officer's cloth belt were to be worn by commissioned officers when the service coat was worn, except when under arms or on field duty. When the officers' belt, M1921, was worn the single shoulder cross-strap passed over the right shoulder and under the shoulder loop on the Service Coat, and was attached to the belt on the left side. The officers' cloth belt could be worn under the conditions for which the M1921 officers' belt was prescribed. The officers' belt, M1921, could be removed when the wearer was indoors.

The Summer Service Coat

A summer coat, khaki colour, of regulation cloth for summer

11

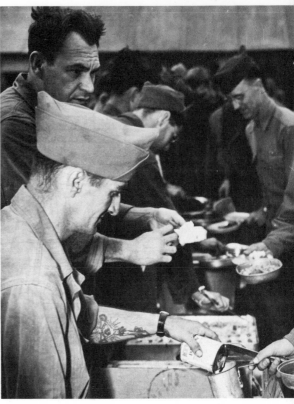

6. **Above left:** *Audie L. Murphy, who died recently in an air crash, was at the age of 20 the most honoured soldier of the US Army in the War, having been awarded every existing individual medal of valour the United States had to offer. He is shown here on the day he was awarded the Congressional Medal of Honor and the Legion of Merit during a parade held at Salzburg, Austria, May 1945. He is wearing the Service Shirt worn in place of the Service coat and displaying both metal and embroidered insignia. The necktie is here shown correctly worn tucked into the shirt. Rank insignia is also shown painted on the front of the M1 steel helmet.*

7. **Below left:** *An example of the pre-1942 black wool tie shown here being worn by Lieutenant-General Courtney H. Hodges, Commander of the 1st US Army, March 1945.*

8. **Above right:** *Technical Sergeant Francis Currey of K Company, 120th Infantry Regt., 30th US Infantry Division, wearing his Congressional Medal of Honor, after the presentation ceremony held at Rheims, France on 27th July 1944. A clear example of the Service Shirt is being worn without the necktie the canvas waist belt and the Garrison cap.*

9. **Below right:** *The issue service shirt worn without the necktie at a Seventh Army memorial day ceremony, May 1945.*

uniforms as stated under 'officers' service breeches' as described below, and of the same design as the white dress coat was authorised for wear by officers with the prescribed summer uniform. The trousers worn with the summer coat were of the same material as the coat.

The Service Shirts
The service shirts were coloured olive-drab of woollen or cotton material. Woollen materials were flannel, worsted and gabardine, 10½ounce in each case. Cotton materials were olive-drab or khaki cotton broadcloth and olive-drab or khaki cotton poplin. Either the olive-drab or the khaki shirt was permitted to be worn when the service coat was worn. Commanding officers could authorise the wearing of the olive-drab or khaki service shirt without the coat. When the shirt was worn, elastic or other armband grips were not allowed to be worn. When the service shirt was worn without the coat, metal or embroidered insignia of grade and collar insignia were worn (see plate 6).

The Issue Necktie
The necktie for officers, warrant officers and enlisted men was of a material without stripe or figure, of olive-drab cotton mohair, of regulation four-in-hand type. Prior to February 1942 the colour of the necktie had been black (plate 7). The necktie was to be worn when the service coat was worn and when the olive-drab wool or khaki shirt was worn without the coat, with the exception that the necktie was not to be worn in the field or under simulated field conditions (plate 8,9). When the shirt was worn without the coat, the necktie was to be tucked into the shirt between the first and second visible buttons (plate 6).

The Trouser Waistbelt
The waistbelt was of olive-drab web 1¼inches in width with a tongueless strap buckle. It was prescribed for wear when the service shirt was worn without the coat. It was permitted to be worn at other times. (See plates 6,8.)

The Service Trousers
The colours, materials and weights of service trousers were the same as described for 'officers' service breeches.' All personnel not specifically authorised to wear breeches were to wear trousers. Personnel authorised to wear breeches could wear trousers when not on duty requiring them to be mounted. Olive-drab (dark shade) service trousers were to be worn by Army officers when in the field and were prescribed for wear by all other Army personnel, olive-drab (dark shade) being the colour prescribed for the service coat. Drab (light shade) service trousers were worn only by officers and could be worn at times other than when in the field. The drab service trousers were an article optional with the individual officer. The light shade coloured trousers (sometimes referred to as Officers' 'Pinks') were advantageous to an officer in that they could be worn with any service coat. (See plates 10,11.) Owing to fading and variations in dyes, the olive-drab dark shade trousers were worn properly only with the service coat made from the same cloth. Officers were advised that for arduous service the trousers issued by the quartermaster to enlisted men and sold to officers were entirely satisfactory for wear. Because of variations in shade, officers were cautioned about wearing these trousers with a standard officers' service coat.

Officers' Service Breeches

The winter uniform provided for two colours: olive-drab (dark shade) and drab (light shade). In both cases the cloth was prescribed as wool, elastique, 18-26 ounce. The darker breeches were required to be worn by officers when in the field. The light shade breeches could be worn by officers at other times and were an article optional with the individual officer. (See plate 4.) The summer uniform provided for breeches of four materials: cotton, khaki, 8.2ounce; rayon, plain weave, 7-8 ounce; cotton warp, mohair filling, khaki; and rayon tropical gabardine. Breeches were worn by officers when on mounted duty. Personnel of animal-mounted, animal-drawn or pack organisations (except pack units of field artillery) were permitted to wear breeches at all times.

The Wool Field Jacket, model 1944

This garment was very similar in apperance to the British Battle-dress blouse, but the cut was much slimmer and the material used was of superior quality (plate 12). This jacket was intended to replace the service coat for all ranks of the Army as a field garment which, being smart enough in appearance, could also be used as a dress item. In practice the troops in the field seldom used the jacket as part of their combat clothing and tended to keep it for use as a dress item for parades and leave. (See plates 10,11.) Its issue was restricted to the European and North African theatres but troops returning to the United States were authorised to wear it in lieu of the service coat.

Stylised Version of the 1944 Field Jacket

A stylised version of the 1944 wool field jacket was sometimes worn by senior US Army officers in the European theatre of operations. Manufactured from the same olive-drab wool material as the 1944 model, this item differed in having two side pockets with slit openings set at an angle to the front of the tunic in place of the two box-pleated patch pockets. The waistband was also slimmer than the other model.

10. Right: *Senior American Commanding Officers seated are (left to right) Generals Simpson, Patton, Spaatz, Eisenhower, Bradley, Hodges, and Gerow. Officers standing are all senior members of the US Army Air Force, Bad Wildungen, Germany 1945.*
11. Below left: *General Patton, second from left and other Generals reviewing the troops of the 10th Armoured Division, Bavaria, July 1945. Both photos show various types of head-dress for General Officers, the difference in colour shades for the uniform jackets and trousers and the variety of footwear permitted to be worn.*
12. Below centre: *Lieutenant General A.M. Patch of the 7th US Army congratulating Captain Carlos C. Odgen on receiving the Congressional Medal of Honour, May 1945. Captain Odgen is wearing the 1944 model wool field jacket.*
13. Below right: *General C. Hodges Commanding General First US Army shown wearing a stylised version of the model 1944 field jacket.*

14. Above left: *US infantry advance towards the Rhine River during an attack from the Colmar Front in eastern France, February 1945. Most of the troops are shown here wearing the long overcoat.*
15. Below left: *Film star Mickey Rooney, visiting the* Ninth Army, eats chow with men of the 102nd Division Service Company at Baeswiler, Germany, February 1945. The soldier at the head of the chow line is wearing the 1942 modified mackinaw coat.
16. Right: *US Army officer's raincoat (left) and belted* trench coat (right) shown here worn under combat conditions. Major-General John W. Leonard (left) commanding general of the 9th Armoured Division, First US Army, and Colonel Adna C. Hamilton, executive officer of the division, watching American

troops crossing the bridge at Remagen, Germany. This was the first bridge over the Rhine to be captured intact by allied forces in the Second World War. Armoured spearheads of the 9th Division made the initial crossing on 7th March 1945.

US Army Overcoats

There were two kinds of Army overcoats: the long overcoat for wear by all ranks, and the short overcoat for use by officers only. Olive-drab cloth of beaver, doeskin, kersey or melton, 26-32 ounce in each case, was prescribed. The buttons were of vegetable ivory or horn, conforming in colour to the material of the coat. Either the long wool overcoat or the short wool overcoat could be worn as standard wear at the option of the individual officer under all conditions. The long overcoat was an issue garment to all enlisted men. The long overcoat was more appropriate in low temperatures, was smarter and more expensive. The short overcoat on the other hand was better suited for active outdoor wear, especially on field service.

The US Army Long Overcoat

The use of the long overcoat by troops in the field as an item of warm combat wear proved to be impracticable. It was too clumsy a garment for effective fighting and in bad weather conditions it quickly became heavy with rain and caked with mud. (See plate 14.) Because of these factors and the introduction of a winter combat uniform it was discarded, its use reverting to that of a dress item.

The US Army Officers' Short Overcoat

The Army officers' short overcoat was an item relatively rare outside of the United States, and tended to be worn as a 'top coat' by senior Army officers and Army generals. It could be worn both with and without the matching cloth belt.

The Modified Mackinaw 1942

This garment was a modification of an earlier item, the Mackinaw 1941. The original short coat was designed primarily for field wear in place of an overcoat. It was manufactured from a heavy canvas duck which was lined with a thick woollen material. It had large pockets to the skirt of the coat and was belted at the waist with an attached cloth belt. The collar to the coat was lined with an artificial fur pile. The modified mackinaw was introduced in 1942 to replace the earlier cumbersome model 1941 coat. The overall weight of this new version was much reduced and in place of the fur pile collar a collar faced with the blanket material was used. (See plate 15.)

The Raincoat for Army Officers

This item of clothing was privately purchased by Army officers and, as such, instructions were given concerning the properties required in a good service type raincoat, including the colour and wearing abilities. The raincoat was to be a waterproof coat of commercial pattern with shoulder loops and as near as practicable olive-drab in colour. Raincoats were to be worn in situations involving exposure to rainy or other inclement weather. A good raincoat was expected to reach to at least below the wearer's knees. It had to stand up to hard, driving rain for long periods without leaking and it had to be made of a strong fabric which resisted tearing. The raincoat was not considered a dress item. Insignia of grade were worn on the shoulder loops. (See plate 16.)

The Raincoat for Enlisted Men

Enlisted men were issued with a raincoat, the design of which had been adopted in 1938 and which, with only minor modifications, remained in service throughout the Second World War. (See plate 17.)

17. **Above left:** *US soldiers attempt to extricate a jeep stuck in deep mud, east of Voellendinger in France, during the winter of 1944. The GI on the left is wearing the enlisted men's raincoat.*

18. **Below left:** *Eisenhower at Julich in 1945. Most of the officers here are wearing the belted trench coat.*

Opposite page : 19. *A two-man Bazooka gun-crew at work during battle training exercises. Both soldiers are wearing the two-piece herringbone twill fatigue suit.*

20. *US troops, all of whom are wearing the two-piece herringbone twill fatigue suit, at work on packing up crates*

The Officer's Trench Coat
The trench coat was not an authorised garment. However, its use was very widespread and, as the garment was sold in many post exchanges, it had at least the semblance of official recognition. It was a useful and practical item since the usual type consisted of a gabardine topcoat treated to be water-repellent, made with belt and shoulder loops, and contained a removable woollen lining. Some manufacturers of the trench coat included a waterproof liner. In temperate climates the trench coat could serve adequately for both warmth and protection from rain. (See plate 18.)

The Two-piece Herringbone Twill Fatigue (Work) Suit, 1942
This two-piece work suit was in olive-drab herringbone twill and was standard issue to all troops in the Army other than mechanics and personnel of armoured units. (See plate 19). From the summer of 1941 it gradually replaced the earlier blue-denim fatigue clothing that had been used throughout the American Army since before the First World War. Although it was primarily intended as a work or fatigue suit it was sometimes used, during the summer months of the war in Europe, as a form of combat clothing (plate 20).

The One-piece Herringbone Twill Suit, 1942 for Mechanics and personnel of Armoured Units

The issue of this one-piece olive-drab herringbone twill 'work uniform' was primarily intended for personnel of armoured units and mechanics in general. However it was used for field instruction (plates 21,22) as well as being adopted as an article of clothing for combat wear during the summer months.

The One-piece Special Herringbone Twill Suit, 1943

This one-piece herringbone twill suit replaced the earlier 1942 pattern suit issued for wear by mechanics and personnel of armoured units. The design of the new suit was different from the 1942 model in that no metal buttons came into contact with the wearer's skin. This change had been necessitated by the many complaints received by the US Army Clothing Authorities from the troops of armoured formations who continually burnt themselves on these buttons. The new suit had an attached cloth belt with buckle and one breast pocket. Sleeve cuffs and trouser leg ends could be buttoned tight to protect the wearer against blast and gas. Like the earlier version, it was sometimes worn as a form of combat clothing.

The Two-piece Herringbone Twill Camouflaged Jungle Suit

Despite this suit being designed primarily for jungle warfare, it was used in a limited way by US Infantry during the early days of the Normandy campaign (plates 23,24). Its use in the European theatre did not last long, however, as the 'jungle' camouflage patterning too closely resembled — in both colouring and shape of camouflage — the combat uniforms worn by troops from the Waffen-SS units. This similarity caused problems of identification, sometimes with fatal results. Its withdrawal from use was also hastened by the introduction in March 1944 of the plain dark-green two-piece suit which had been designed to replace the 'jungle' suit.

---

21. Above left: *A two-man mortar crew under field instruction during battle training with live ammunition, held to prepare American forces in Britain for the forthcoming invasion of the Continental mainland. All three soldiers in the picture are wearing the one-piece herringbone twill suit. The weapon in use is a 60mm M2 mortar.*

22. Below left: *The one-piece herringbone twill suit, worn here by a technical sergeant demonstrating a portable flame-thrower to officer candidates at a US Army School Centre in Britain during August 1943.*

23, 24. Right: *Two pictures of the two-piece herringbone twill camouflage jungle suit. Plate 23 shows infantry studying the position of their next objective during advances in western Normandy near Pont Brocard. Plate 24 shows engineers clearing rubble from an alley in Canisy, France, (which had been bombed the preceding night) to make way for armoured vehicles. Limited use was made of these camouflaged combat suits in the European Theatre of Operations. During the early stages of the Normandy fighting they proved to be too similar in both colour and pattern to the camouflaged combat suits worn by units of the German Waffen-SS — the result meant errors in identifying American troops that sometimes proved fatal. The jungle camouflage suits were eventually replaced by the plain dark-green two-piece combat suits.*

The M1941 Field Jacket
The material used in the manufacture of this field jacket was cotton cloth, olive-drab in colour, wind-resistant and water-repellent and lined with shirting flannel. The garment was provided with shoulder loops. The field jacket was authorised for wear by officers, warrant officers and enlisted men as prescribed for the service coat, with the provision that the use of the field jacket on ceremonial or special occasions, or on furlough or pass, was permitted or forbidden within the discretion of the senior local commander. The design of the M1941 field jacket was based broadly on the lines of a civilian wind-jacket (plates 25, 26). It became increasingly unpopular with the American troops, proving inadequate under adverse weather conditions, especially in winter, and was finally superseded by the introduction of the M1943 field jacket (plate 27).

The M1943 Field Jacket and Trousers
This combat outfit, consisting of a four-pocket tunic and trousers of matching olive-drab water-repellent and windproof cotton material was introduced for universal service with combat formations from 1943 onwards. (See plate 27.) It replaced the earlier M1941 field jacket which, after its initial use in the European theatre, had proved to be unsuitable in the field under combat conditions. The M1943 field jacket was suitable for combat in mild weather and when worn with a pile fabric liner provided the wearer with adequate protection against more severe winter conditions (plate 28). When circumstances permitted the newly designed olive-drab cotton peaked field cap was worn with this uniform, and in 1944 a specially designed hood (see below) was issued for wear with the jacket (plate 29). New style combat boots, similar in design to US Airborne parachute boots, were issued to infantry troops and were intended to be worn as part of the complete M1943 field uniform (plates 10, 11).

The M1944 Hood, worn in conjunction with the M1943 Combat Jacket
This particular item of issue clothing was designed to be worn over all other forms of military headdress including the steel helmet (plate 29), but it was possible for it to be worn under the helmet (plate 49). It was worn with the M1943 combat or field jacket and was buttoned on to the jacket by using the top button on the front of the coat and the buttons to the shoulder loops. It could also be fitted for wear to the officer's trench coat.

The Wool Knit High Neck Sweater
This long-sleeved garment when introduced became a general issue field item. It could be worn over the flannel shirt or under the combat jacket where its use supplemented the pile liner to the M1943 combat jacket. It was machine knitted from dark olive-drab wool and could be worn buttoned up at the neck. (See plate 28.)

25. **Above left:** *The M1941 field combat jacket. This garment was eventually replaced by the more practical M1943 field jacket.*
26. **Above right:** *Rear view of the M1941 field jacket. Using a portable stove, US troops cook a meal in a Cherbourg street, June 1944.*

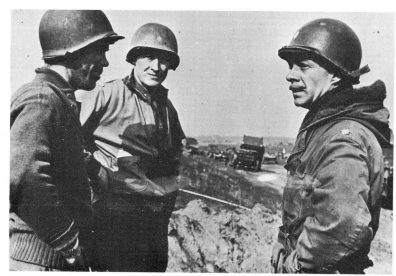

27. **Centre left:** *Major-General Allison J. Barnett (centre) Commanding General, 10th Infantry Division, conferring with fellow officers from the 274th Infantry Regiment in a street in Rochershausen, Germany, immediately after the crossing of the Saar River by troops of the 70th Division. All are wearing the model 1943 field jackets. Lieutenant-Colonel Landstrom of 274th Infantry Regiment (second from left) is wearing standard pattern leather gloves.*
28. **Centre right:** *The M1943 field jacket (right) worn here with a pile fabric liner and (left) the wool-knit high neck sweater.*
29. **Below:** *US Combat Engineers under enemy fire push a section of a Bailey bridge into place to span the river Ill near Niederehnheim, France. The soldier in the centre is wearing the M44 hood attached to his combat jacket and worn over his helmet.*

30. Below left: *An example of the officer's quality helmet liner with its rounded thicker rim worn under the standard issue M1 helmet.*

31. Above: *The US M1 steel helmet and liner worn here by a soldier demonstrating the anti-tank Bazooka weapon during invasion exercises in England. Of interest also are the Army issue goggles, worn here to supplement the blast screen at the muzzle of the rocket launcher.*

32. Below centre: *American Undersecretary of War Robert P. Patterson, during a visit to Erwitte, Germany, shakes hands with one of the platoon leaders of the guard of honour provided for him by troops of the 95th Infantry Division, 9th US Army, on 4th May 1945. The honour guard are all wearing helmet liners in place of the steel helmet.*

33. Below right: *Helmet liners used as headgear during US training manoeuvres. This is an early 'posed' photograph to show the new 'Bazooka' rocket launcher.*

US Army Headgear
Commanding officers could prescribe the wearing of such authorised headgear as was appropriate under the existing combat or weather conditions.

The Service Cap
The prescribed material for wear with the winter uniform was wool, elastique, olive-drab (dark shade), 18-26ounce. With the summer uniform, it could be of cotton, khaki, or tropical worsted khaki material. It was authorised for wear by all officers, warrant officers and enlisted men (plate 10).

The US M1 Steel Helmet and Helmet Liner
The helmet and liner worn together comprised an article of issue authorised for wear by all personnel. The US M1 steel helmet was introduced in 1942, replacing the helmet that had been used by the US Army since 1917 and which closely resembled the British pattern steel helmet. The helmet liner was a separate item, matching the shape of the steel helmet and was normally worn together with the helmet. It was manufactured from a lightweight compressed fibre. Two types of liner existed: the officer's pattern which had a thicker, more rounded rim and was finished with a covering of olive-drab fine gauze material, and the type issued to all other personnel in the Army which was of the same basic shape and colouring but had a sharp rim and a smoother olive-drab painted finish. (See plates 30,31.) This fine distinction between the two types of helmet liners did not always apply in the field as many officers used what in effect had been intended for enlisted men. The helmet liner was permitted to be worn by all ranks on those occasions, normally ceremonial or non-combat guard duty, calling for the steel helmet but not requiring the wearer's head to be protected by the helmet. The helmet liner was also used in field training. (See plates 32,33.)

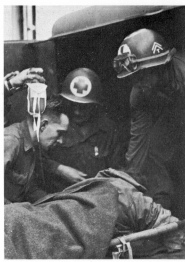

Helmet Markings

These were strictly regulated but it is evident that usage in the
field resulted in a fairly wide range of different markings.
Military Police were distinguished both in the field and in the
United Kingdom by a number of methods, their white painted
helmets or helmet liners giving rise to their popular nickname
'snowdrops'. (See plates 4,5,34.) US Army doctors and medics
were identified in the field in a number of ways, one of which
was the display of the Red Cross sign painted on the steel helmet. The design of these crosses tended to vary from unit to
unit.(See plates 35, 36.) The same applied to the helmet liner.
Rank insignia was also painted on the steel helmet (plates 6,
16, 35), generals being permitted to affix — or paint — small
five-pointed gold stars to either the helmet or the liner (plate
10). Helmet camouflage was normally provided by the use of an
olive drab or green helmet net worn over the steel helmet and
occasionally garnished with sacking (plate 37).

The Garrison Cap

The prescribed materials, both summer and winter, are as stated
for the service cap. The garrison cap (formerly the 'field' or
'overseas cap') was authorised for wear by all Army personnel.
It was piped for general officers in cord braid of gold bullion,
rayon or metallised cellophane of gold colour (plate 38). Other
Army officers wore cord braid of gold bullion, rayon or metallised cellophane with black silk intermixed. The Garrison cap
was piped for enlisted men in coloured cording, depending on
the wearer's arm of service, the infantry being light blue.

The Field Hat, cotton, khaki

The prescribed material was cotton, khaki, 8—12ounce. It was
authorised for wear by all officers and enlisted men except
those of mounted units and of overseas (outside the United
States) departments. The brim was to be worn turned down all
round the hat (plate 19).

The M1941 Wool Knit Cap

The M1941 wool knit cap was for wear by officers, warrant-
officers and enlisted men. It was olive-drab, wool knit, of
a standard adopted design with curtain and visor. It could be
worn as a woollen cap by itself (plate 39) or under the steel
helmet and helmet liner.

34, 35, 36. Above: *Military
Police helmet markings for
use in the field differed
from the white-painted
helmets sometimes used by
American patrols in the UK.
Plate 34 shows a three-man
military police patrol team
seated in a jeep mounted
with a .50 calibre M2HB
Browning heavy machine-gun.
35: Medical personnel were
readily identified by having
Red Cross markings painted
onto their steel helmets.
36: Another version of the
Red Cross identification
markings.*

37. Above left: *In a foxhole near Caumont in France a GI enjoys a 'K' ration dinner. He is wearing the M1 steel helmet camouflaged with netting and garnished with sacking strips.*
38. Above right: *The General officer's version of the Garrison cap. General Omar Bradley (left) Commanding General, 12th US Army Group, with staff officers at Frankfurt airport in July 1945.*
39. Below: *A 60mm mortar crew in training at a US Army Command Camp in Britain. The three-man crew are all wearing the M1941 wool-knit cap, shown here worn as a separate item of headgear.*

40. **Above left:** *The wool-knitted toque worn under the M1 steel helmet. A patrol makes its report by means of a portable wireless set, as allied ground forces enter Cologne in March 1945.*

41, 42. **Above right and below left:** *The olive-drab canvas leggins, worn by officer candidates on an assault course in Britain*

and by a GI sharing his candy bar with a little French girl in June 1944.
43. Below right: *Tackling a German road block. The GI on the right is wearing Army leather field boots, with the built-in gaiters.*

The Wool Knitted Toque
This item was a standard item of winter wear. Knitted in olive-drab coloured wool in the same fashion as the British Army 'Balaclava Helmet' it could be worn under the steel helmet (plate 40).

The Lambskin Lined Winter Cap
The prescribed material was olive-drab serge. This item of Army headgear was authorised for wear by personnel in Alaska or other cold winter localities.

The Winter Cap
The material used for the manufacture of this item of headgear was olive-drab duck. It was authorised for wear in northern climates.

The Service Hat
This item was sometimes referred to as the 'Campaign Hat'. The material was beaver coloured felt. Personnel were required to wear the hat with a leather chin strap five-eighths of an inch in width. It was authorised for wear by members of mounted units, by troops in Alaska, in overseas departments, and in cooler localities where the cotton uniform was not worn, and by officers when the field hat was worn by enlisted men. The service hat proved to be an unwieldly item of dress and was discarded in 1941. It was therefore an item of dress that did not make a general appearance in the European theatre of operations.

US Army Footgear
The adopted shade of all leather in clothing, footwear and articles of equipment, except as noted, was known as 'Army russet'.

Officer's Dress Boots
Army russet leather of commercial pattern without lacing. Officers who were required to be mounted were to wear boots when on mounted duty. Personnel of animal-mounted, animal-drawn or pack organisations (except pack units of field artillery) could wear boots at all times.

Shoes
Commercial pattern, high or low, Army russet leather. Low shoes could be worn with plain tan (or brown) socks by officers and enlisted men when authorised by the commanding officer. (See plate 10.)

Officer's Field Boots
Army russet leather, leggins to pattern, with three buckles on the side or with laces. Although certain officers — General Patton in particular — appeared to prefer this style of footwear (plate 10) the officer's field boot was gradually replaced by the newly designed high-laced 'combat boot' (plate 10). These new boots were introduced for wear by all arms during 1943.

The Olive-Drab Canvas Leggins
These were of adopted standard and design. Worn with high shoes by all officers and enlisted men except those of animal-mounted, animal-drawn or pack organisations (except pack units of field artillery) when prescribed by the commanding officer (plates 20,41,42). The olive-drab lace-on canvas leggins formed part of the complete M1941 field or combat uniform. When this style of dress was superseded by the introduction of

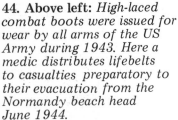

44. Above left: *High-laced combat boots were issued for wear by all arms of the US Army during 1943. Here a medic distributes lifebelts to casualties preparatory to their evacuation from the Normandy beach head June 1944.*

45. Above centre left: *A shot showing the olive-drab wool muffler, worn by the PFC on the right and rubber overshoes worn by the PFC changing the wheel of the jeep.*

46. Above centre right: *The wool-knit muffler and wool and leather gloves worn by a soldier (left) from the 117th US Infantry Regiment clearing German snipers from a house in the Belgian town of Stavelot.*

47. Above far right: *Major-General Hugh Gaffey, of the 4th US Armored Division, confers with Lieutenant-Colonel Jaques (right) who directed leading elements in the attack on Ginsdorf in March 1945. The General is wearing army russet leather boots and leather gloves; Colonel Jaques holds a pair of wool-knit mittens.*

the M1943 combat uniform the canvas leggins were replaced first by leather boots with a form of built-in gaiters (plate 43) and later by the newly designed high-lace combat boots, issued for wear by all arms and services and similar in appearance to the US Paratroopers' boots. (See plates 10,44.)

Rubber Boots
Russet, waterproof, commercial pattern rubber boots could be worn when conditions made their use necessary, when prescribed by commanding officers of posts, camps, or stations and of mine planters, cable ships, and transports.

Overshoes
When conditions warranted their use, overshoes could be prescribed by the commanding officer. (See plate 45.)

The Olive-Drab Wool Muffler
The wool knit olive-drab muffler was for optional wear when an overcoat was worn. It was also used by troops in combat during cold weather (plates 45,46).

US Army Service Gloves
Service gloves were of leather or wool or a combination of both.

Leather and Wool Service Gloves:
Olive-drab wool material was used for the backs to these service gloves, with russet leather to the palms and fingers and snap fasteners to the wrists. They were issued to personnel of all arms and services. (See plate 46.)

Wool knit olive-drab mittens were also known to have been worn (plate 47).

Wool Knit Service Gloves:
Wool knit gloves were olive-drab. They were worn by officers

and men when prescribed and were optional when off duty. (See plate 21.)

Leather Service Gloves:
The leather gloves were of light russet leather, lined or unlined, and were of the snap fastener, pull-on or buckle type. They were worn by officers and men of mounted organisations and officers of all other arms when prescribed, and were optional when off duty (plate 27).

Web Field Equipment
The standardised web field equipment for officers consisted of the belt, pistol or revolver, M1912, the suspenders and pistol or revolver belt, M1936.

Officers' Sidearms
In the field the pistol (or revolver) with holster and 21 rounds of ammunition was worn by officers and warrant officers. It was not worn by chaplains, and was only worn by officers of the medical department when necessary for personal protection.

Identification Tags
Identification tags (sometimes referred to as 'Dog Tags') were worn by each member of the Army at all times, with either uniform or civilian clothing and were to be removed temporarily only as the necessities of personal hygiene required. One tag was to be suspended from the neck underneath the clothing by a cord, tape or thin chain 40inches in length, passed through a small hole in the tag, with the second tag fastened about 2½inches above the first on the same cord, tape or chain, both tags held securely in place. These embossed tags were prescribed as part of the uniform and were habitually worn by the owner, being issued to each member of the Army as soon as practicable after entry into service. (See plate 48.)

48: *US identification tags, prescribed to be worn by all members of the American armed forces at all times. These tags were embossed with the soldier's name, Army number, religion, information regarding any innoculations and the blood type of the wearer.*

31

49. *Medics from the 94th U.S. Infantry Division wearing vest-like Red Cross markers. These vests, made by women of the French Red Cross, were issued to American medical troops in answer to the German claim that German troops could not tell the difference between medical personnel and regular infantry owing to insufficient identification markings. The contrast between the old arm-band identification and the new Red Cross vests is clearly shown here. The use of the M44 hood worn under the M1 steel helmet is shown in this photo being worn by the soldier on the left.*

50. Right: *A typical view of U.S. infantry combat equipment. Troops being briefed prior to the crossing of the river Roer, Germany, February 1945.*